Love n Politics

Theodore Parker

Acknowledgments

I first, and foremost would like to thank The Creator of all. God gives us obstacles throughout our journey, for which we are being tested on our faith. On this pathway, we are given angels to provide direction for which we need to go and be in life. We also have to become angels for people who need our guidance and love's energy, to help them as well. Which makes me very appreciative for the people placed in my life through this journey whether long term or short term.

A big shout out goes to the amazing woman who believed in my dreams, the queen herself (as told to print), Mercedez Santana. She provided the visual for the book cover *Love n Politics.* A big part of this project is credited to Philena Alford for giving me direction and the steps needed to make this possible. Nicole Custard plays a part in this because she always told me I had a gift. But I lacked resources, capital, and that drive needed to make this dream become a reality. I also want to give a huge shout out to my daughter Carmen. I'm just shouting her out because I can and she's my princess. I do this for her. Everyone needs a "no" person. Beonka Robinson takes this title because she helps with decisions needed and not needed, to make this collection of literature deem worthy for the public.

As you can see, I'm only shouting out women. Fellas it is very important that you leave the "bros before hoes" mentality behind. Women have the ability to shape and mold a man's character for the better, when they notice that man trying to change the world. They have a natural instinct for this. Plus they are smarter, smell better and pleasing to the eye. And in no way shape or form I'm calling any of these queens a hoe.

Lastly, the biggest part of this whole creations goes to my inspiration. That one special lady, that kept my mind on her. To where I can admit I was going crazy over. In order to control and express these feelings, I decided to write and write some more. I can't say that it helped the situation, but *Love n Politics* is the outcome. Thank you R.B. She's so dope.

Preface

To be human is difficult. Different versions of what others choose to call life are ran through our eyes at different times. We then must pick and choose what stimulates our energy from those encounters. It's the borrowing of other energies that establishes a self-identity within our own, to satisfy our spirit and heart. Within all these different perceptions, the one common thing is love.

Love has no bounds. We take limitless steps to get recognition from people we deeply care about. Love has no rules. We will cheat, lie, manipulate, and deceive, to win the heart of the ones we choose to pursue. I am personally not a fan of these approaches. I am a strong believer in karma. To achieve love correctly, will have a better and more positive end results. Love is infinite. Ultimate love has sacrificed human life. People throughout history have killed, or given their lives for the sake of love. Love can come with pain and tears, but it's a feeling that we all desire to feel as if it can be an addiction. I live off a creed a musical artist says: *"If you not down to die about it, you don't love it"*

To be political. Everyone has an opinionated political view on how the world needs to be run or ran. From global policies all the way to community, the discussion to enforce is called politics. It can be drawn up pages of paperwork or oral communications, but there has to be an agreement to a conflict. I am not a huge fan of the trickledown effect, so my politics come from my culture and heritage. In the truest form of honesty, I feel my DNA's origin is lost and scattered. With that said we have to base our being on intuition. I feel like some of the things we do as a culture are not correct to have a positive long lasting affect for our future. Along said, there are significant, beautiful people throughout history who has attempted to open our eyes that gave us dignity and self-worth. They gave us a feeling to hold our heads high, and recognize our beauty.

My reason for *Love n Politics* is simple. I was on a military deployment thinking of ways to change myself and become a better person. I needed to find multiple ways to generate income to give my family a better future. My only niche I know is the ability to help people mentally and physically giving them a spiritual boost. In the military, we deal with different people from all walks of life, and from every corner of the world. I would offer advice through relatable stories of my own, to help with the mental. On the physical side, people would come work out with me, and learn how to obtain a healthy body. Given the fact I am considered Mr. 300 the PT Stud, I didn't mind showing them physical activities. The best way to help others become better is to teach, but more importantly to lead.

At the same time, I was fighting my own personal heart. It was a feeling to feel, but the need to be still. Let's just say someone ran off with my heart, and to gain it back in the most civilized form was to write. There is a thin line between love and crazy. This woman possesses every attribute that a man such as myself desires. She is not made for every man. She can be too much, only because you cannot come at her with bullshit. You have to come all the way legit, and be prepared plus patient for a long journey ahead. I would say she is the female version of me. A black woman has to know that her worth is ten times more valuable than any jewel. This is the one secret I know, which drew me to her because she knows herself too.

On that note, I am here to change the world through relatable emotions. To give dialogue that needs to be passed through our mouths. This collection of literature gives us strength to become better individuals to our loved ones, our community, and ourselves. I base my world off truths. Honesty is the ultimate form of freedom. My people's biggest need is to have freedom. It has to start with the truth. No cover-ups, nothing in the dark. One of the things I have been trying to achieve for quite some time now. The saying goes: The truth will either make you smile or cry. Smile with me. Cry with me. Love with me. Politic with me.

Love

Her Touch

Cosmic air... starlight's

Fusion of life

Chemistry strong

Binding to be right

Math equation on the chalkboard

M squared the speed of light

But that black hole's grip

Will have everything stuck

With no escape

But my origins darkness

Makes me give no fucks

It's your touch

Far Away

There has been a distance between us

Not mental

But the actual physical

Many miles away

I can still feel her energy

She's not a believer

But I'm going to change her heart

Our energies don't lie

For mines holds you

It touches your forehead with mine

My hand on the small of your back

And any place she's willing to open her energy to

This is out of love not lust

She's learning how to trust

I am the convincer of her

At the same time she fixes me

Perfect imperfections

Another mold is form

It brings us closer mentally

I pray for her

I feel her praying for me

Pray she reaches her dreams

I pray I don't ever stop loving my queen

The Beautiful Dream (Part 1.)

Facing each other laying on their sides

They were silent the whole time just bonding eyes

Then she lets a subtle n quiet sigh

"What's wrong love" he replies

She said she doesn't want to awake from this dream

He gave her self-esteem she's on a different high

Addicted

Plus when his dick's inside, it feels like a high tide swept underneath

Her heart pounds as she breathes deep

He puts his hand on her chest to feel the beep

She then starts to cry

He says,

"Baby I dreamt of these days long before you" "I couldn't sleep because I would constantly think of you" "The key to my heart is chained to your belt loop" "I'm forever true to you" "Just looking at you makes me never want to close my eyes" " You say that you don't want to wake up from this dream well neither do I"

He draws closer, their foreheads touch

The real definition of energy's love and how to brain fuck

She arouses from anywhere and anyplace on her body he decides to touch

It doesn't take much

The definition of ultimate trust

She is secure like cage bars

The Beautiful Dream (Part 2.)

She is secure like cage bars

When her cage opens she has unleashed a beast

That feasts on lust, but she's particular

She eats particular meat

That meat is he,

And this isn't that weak granny kiss bullshit, peck on the cheek

She wants all of he

So she releases all her energy

Today she leads, rolls on top of him with a hard straddle

She wants it now

The decision is made, as if the judge hits the gavel

Let it be known that her pussy is the best

She slid down on him because he is fully erect

Both of her hands on his chest

Slow and hard

Slow and hard

Slower, harder

HARDER!

SLOWER!

His left hand on her thigh

The right hand on her neck

He is still an alpha male

But that is why she chose him

She doesn't do, nor is she attracted to the frail

"Cum baby" he whispers

"I'm Cumming!" she yells

She locks up

Her water streams as she deeply inhales

He is still an alpha male, and turns her to her back

Gives her what she needs

It pleases him to please her

It has to be satisfaction guaranteed

She's about to orgasm again is what he sees

Mission accomplished and at the same time
releases his seeds

The long pause

All you can hear, them breathing

Both parties are pleased

Love over lust is what paints better birds and bees

Love n Politics from a king and his queen

"See you in my sleep"

Trust Me

You run from me, it's because you love hard

To love someone as hard as we do

Comes with great sacrifice and vulnerability

But do you dare to be brave?

The spoken, but unspoken trust

Jump out, and I'll catch you

Trust me?

To Destroy Love

To destroy love

Outside opposing forces

The obstruction of justice rather "just us"

It's just us, but then, here comes such n such

Such n such has a negative gut

Because she made bad decisions when she was young

And she can't own up

With the fact that she laid with shit

So every nigga "ain't" shit

Which means this loyal nigga "ain't" shit

This real life in the flesh protector

Mr. Trilla by the 100%

God fearing Pharoah "ain't" it

Because he had a choice to choose between the two

And that bitch Miss Negative Gut was the hit and miss

Whispers into her friends ear a bunch of fake fabricated false sneak disses

But it's always a snake near and she has a tongue split... hiss

But Mrs. Trilla "ain't" hearing it

Her favorite seasoning is called Check a Bitch Quick

No salt added or rather thrown

Because this cloth's cut is from a strong fabric

The tag says Made in the Himalaya free from static

Her Warrior

Recovering from a long journey

He paces slow

From slaying dragons and long battles from the enemy

His body is tired but the heart says different

He's determined

For he longs for reuniting

She feels the same

Her warrior is the truth

He's a leader, and he is fearless

She knows his protection has no bounds

He will die for her

She feels blessed that he has made room for that sacrifice

For he is loyal

Head up, chin up, standing straight

Chivalry still has a pulse because of him

Only to teach the youth to love

An important necessity to life

To Be Patient

Because he is impatient but,

He's patiently waiting

Debating necessary strategies

The statistics to get this

Probability has to be efficient

He has to be strategic

His strategy to knock out all competition

And to separate against them

Impatiently waiting for her to give in

Speaking his success into existence

Her essence

Her presence

Being patient is the lesson

He is out of his element

This is his confession

In his ear buds,

You can hear Usher's "Confessions"

He is her "Superstar"

Her "Seduction" is effortless

Like Tiger Woods to a par

But it's a tight lid to a jar

It's hard for him to get a grip on life

To be patient is hard

But it's worth the sacrifice

Sunday's Love

Dream with me...

Sunday morning's wake up

She opens her nose

Her eyes are still closed

The vibe from last night though

Had her in a sense of complete whole

It was just dinner and wine

And perfect conversation from a divine Pharoah

Royalty plush...

No bullshit, no toilet flush

She opens her eyes to clear that buzz

She's aroused... The reason why

Because it smells like Waffle House mixed with Grandmoma's house

She hears him coming

So she pretends to be sleep

He knows she is faking, gives her a kiss on her cheek

Then opens her eyes

Her sweet voice, it gives off an innocent "huh", "what"

That royal nigga explains "Baby sit up"

"I got what you need early morning for the gut"

"We need to decide if we're going to sneak to church"

Breakfast in bed, scrambled eggs, plus grits

Toast with strawberry jam

So she can stay thick

Not a fan of swine, but we got bacon just two strips

A light-weight mimosa to sip, she licks her hungered lips

She doesn't get full, but the queen is satisfied

And so they dialogue about hearing God's word

To get dressed, they decide

The intent is not to impress

But they keep it so OG, mixed with her finesse

It doesn't take long for him, so he waits sitting on the edge of the bed

And he watches her move, thanking the Lord for the way they've met

It took him some time

She wasn't an easy catch

He had to king the fuck up

But it made him stronger

She is in the closet, trying to decide

And she notices him staring

She poses harder intentionally,

She has on panties and thighs

She wears a bra and a stomach

She is fresh out of the shower

He patiently waits,

It's probably going to take another hour

He doesn't mind, no

Because to him, it's like a private show

He wishes there was a remote control every time she puts on her lotion... Slow motion

She's like, "Whaaaaat" showing dimples and teeth

He smirks out an "O.K."

But Miss Parker knows what she is doing

Like the water hose scene on Friday

"Baby we're going to be late" "And if you smile that way again, I'm pouncing you like a lion's steak" "Hurry up and put your clothes on" "My dick is growing strong from boiling testosterone"

Which takes over by the bulk

He is controlled crazy

But he wants to turn into the Incredible Hulk

She says, "Feel but be still"

She came with jokes

Somewhat knowing that she might not come out of that closet from his hard stroke

"I rock the boat, I'm not just anybody" like Aaliyah quotes

She puts on a skirt, its calf length long

(Pause)

To the reader: You know how I know she's fine?

Because she puts on more clothes, and he still catches a hard on

(Continue)

He says, "Let me help you find a shirt"

It's just a cop out to get closer to her, you damn right he's a flirt

They scan through her side of the closet rack

He presses up on her from the back

As if he is teaching her how to shoot pool or play golf

And he doesn't know how to play any of that

He inhales the back of her neck

He fucked up, now he's fully erect

She says "stooooop", but she doesn't mean that shit

She bumps him with her ass real sexy, then pokes out her hip

He returns back to her waist with a firmer grip

She turns around, the slow attack of her lips

This is love 101, Chapter 4

I can't get enough like J. Cole

Ten minutes later... Yeah I said ten!

He's a situational lover, so the situation depends

They don't have time

They have shit to do

Compared to last night it was like making The Titanic and Forest Gump 2 (long ass movies)

So now they're moving fast

Re-wash their asses and change clothes but don't forget the cash

He says, "Dear Lord forgive us, but we're not bad"
"This is my wife and it's your fault because you

created that" "Can we sneak in while they're singing along"

With sarcasm God replies, "Sure I might be able to do that"

They open the church door and it's a loud squeaky crack

He angrily whispers, "All this money they make at this church, and they…"

Never mind that

She looks at him, with that don't be ugly look

Man! This girl fine

Walking in church, every eye turns back by the masses

God has jokes too

They catch the last row, trying hard not laugh

Holds her hand the whole time because he's whole with her

She's his math

Amen

Her Corner

To be in her corner

Waiting on the bell to ring

Ding! Ding! Ready to knock down anything and everything

She's my butterfly and I'm the sting

Bob n weave these haters just don't Bob n weave me

To be in her corner if she needs me

Starring down opponents from the other side of this boxing ring

Black trunks with HER PITBULL spelled in gold trim

Black gloves with the initials R.B. at the hymn

To be in her corner

To Feel Safe and Secure (Protected)

This girl is a blessing

She's showing me lessons, my vision is clear

Big up my chest

Less aggression towards my peers

No half stepping

Whatever she needs, no need to question

I work hard for her like a warehouse full of Mexicans

The new perception

Push it hard like school bullies

She makes me better, Fab and Ne-Yo, cranks to pulleys

Which means this is a machine

Don't let these ratchets throw in their wrenches

She fine tuned

I'm going to kill that pussy, like I am a henchman

The only purpose is to fill up her purse and make her purr

It's not a problem

I'm on my paper, and I'm packing girth

Wet her up, like murk men

Stains to shirts

Roll up a blunt

And then lay up until she curtains

Laying up, like I'm Ice Man

Mr. George Gervin

My finger rolls to her hoop, so smooth that she purrs again

Love Art

Beautiful the night

From the artistic sight

Feeds the cancer's appetite

His pencil strikes the blank page

She has a nature's insight

Wombman

Mixed with the cosmic light

To be quiet, but her vision, a powerful mite

The fruit becomes ripe

Drink Her

Give me the whole bottle with an unbroken seal

Hell no! I'm not passing this bottle, ain't nobody got time for that

When it comes to her, I don't want a mere sip

So I was told to not be thirsty

This is far beyond thirst; I call it hungry for my Hershey

You titled me thirsty huh,

Well I want to drink her, slurp her

Like its 100 degrees and she's my Slurpee

Drink her until I'm no longer sober

Drink her because her essence and energy's cup runneth over

Drink her fruit juice

Let it flow down my chin

There is no coming up for air

I'm too thirsty to catch my wind

Deep-sea dive like flippers and fins

With nothing fishy down here, sweeter than cinnamon

Brown skin, brown skin

That pretty pink within

A blessing to kiss those lips to where all creation begins

I am Pharoah

So when it comes to her, I don't want a mere sip

Pillow Talk

(Slang)

U got these guys quick to say

"Pillow talk no way"

"Pillow talkn is soft"

"Pillow talkn is gay"

(Pause)

Say what!

You're mad at the fact that I enjoy to lay up

After I released my nut

Which puts me in a lightweight paralysis while smoking a blunt

Puff

And she rolled it for me

She wiped my balls with that warm towel

But I'm living foul?

I didn't have to ask her to fix me a sandwich, with fruit punch and Crunch n Munch

Getting ready for the next beat the beat up, strong arm Andrew Luck

Say what!?

You damn right

I will pillow talk

I will chop it up with my sheets

Give my blanket a speech

Have a great debate with my mattress

And sing a melody to my box spring

Pillow talk bitch!

Because I don't feel like getting up

This lady fine as fuck

Got ass? Just enough

Got breast? A hand full of seduction to cup and
nipple suck

More than enough

And you mad because I choose to lay up

Before a dunk

Pillow Talk

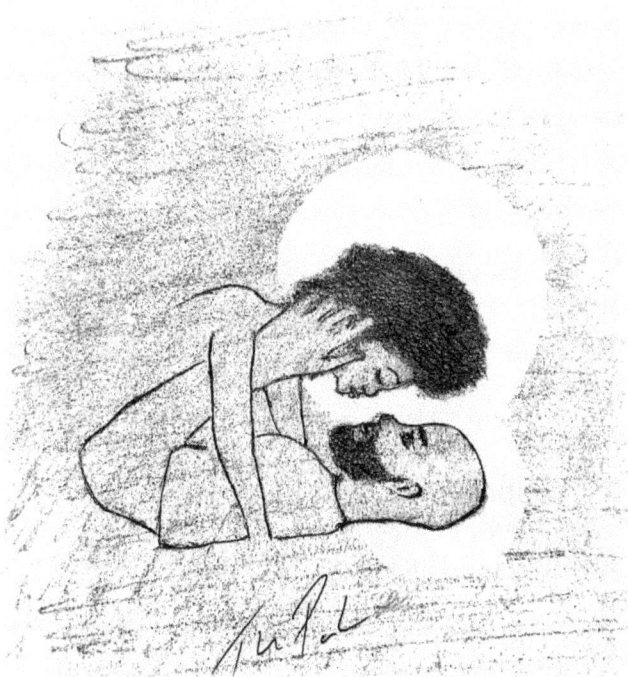

The Best Moment of the Day

The best moment of the day

To cherish time

Seconds to minutes

Can last a lifetime

The best moment of the day

Because everything surrounding was hell

She and He are not bossed up yet

Subordinates vs. insubordinates

The energies of misery run through the workforce

But the clock must tic to an end

The best moment of the day

But first comes the punch out

Then comes traffic

They come home to each other

They cleanse their soul first

He washes her back

He inhales her face towel like Tony Montana's coke mountain

She laughs and calls him nasty

Wine is poured the music is soulful

It's his turn to cook

The main ingredient that got her hooked

Crab legs, shrimp, and corn on the cob, with the little red potatoes

Cuffing season was a while ago

Only for...

The best moment of the day

He can tell by her look

That sexy seductive bite on her lip

When she walks down the hall, she gives an extra switch

Look how she can't be still

Like she has to go pee

But that energy is coming from the same place

And at the same time, you have to keep it cool

Ain't no hard dicks at this dinner table?

We can't burn up the food

She turns him on

Everything about her from head to toe

She's not even dressing sexy

But that natural brown hair

And those pretty teeth

Lips of an Egyptian queen

It's a comfortable Tuesday

V-neck, T-shirt, and no bra

Short shorts

PT shorts with the swimming trunk net cut out

They're loose but let that shit ride

And if the energy is high he can pull them to the side

Only because,

It's the best moment of the day

He tells her, "Later for you"

She replies, "Only if the food is good"

Dessert is on their minds

They sit at the table

She silently blesses both plates

He listens to her about her day

She listens to him back

"Fuck them haters" is what they both say

3rd glass of wine

No more for tonight

She was waiting to inhale

He rolls one tight

Plus two episodes of Martin

Everything is right, right? Do you know why?

It's the best moment of the day

They put it out halfway

They were already mind fucking

They are way past 12 play

Mixed with album 12 play

Fireworks to homeruns

Take me out to the ball game

Now time for shower number 2

Which turns into scene 2

Converting to air conditioning and thick blankets

She rubs his warehouse back

He rubs her medical field calves and feet

All the way until she falls asleep

The best moment of the day

Turned into night

He finishes the ashtray

The clouds make her dream better

He knows what she needs

She longs to be held

He longs to hold her

But first...

He makes sure the doors are locked

Switches his selector from safe to semi

For they are now safe

Only 5 hours to be human

And then back to 19 hours of robot slavery

The alarm clock is set

The sick and tired of being sick and tired is on pause

For tomorrow is another day

And they both cannot wait

They will wake up with smiles on their faces

To look forward to

Another best moment of the day

Good night

Share My Thoughts

Who can say that they wake up to poetry?

Numerous words put together

Puzzled in pieces?

To express one's feelings for you

With similes and metaphors

For she is the thesis

Even the corny ones... For example

(Life's an ironing board, I am the pants, which makes u the iron, her steam I can't withstand)

So what's the point?

Think of me, when you first wake up

Think of me, like the way I think of you

Think of me queen

Think of your king

Because I am thinking of you

I think about how you rest your head

I think about how you lay in bed

About what you are wearing

Even the type of wrap on your head

I think of the day, you having me say, "I do"

Do you think of me baby, how I think of you

Politics

Whys on Top of Why

I have to teach my kids the word "racists"

Talk about the tears to a face

Innocence only knows love

Something we were naturally born to do

How do you respond to them?

What do you say?

Giving our children reasons on why others were
taught to hate

Whys on top of why

Without Us

Where would this country be without us?

Would life be slower?

Did we speed life up?

Frederick McKinley made a claim

We need to transport meat

He gave us the refrigerated truck

The rotating dial phone was slow

Shirley Ann Jackson said make that bitch touch-tone

She wasn't finished by any means

She gave us call waiting and caller I.D.

Valeri Thomas worked for NASA, and performed many experiments and solutions

So give thanks because she gave us 3-Dimensional illusions

Open your eyes and kill the idea of 40 ounces and Cadillacs

Patricia Bath gave us Laserphaco Probe for treating cataracts

Do you know Charles Richard Drew?

Gave us a blood bank, who would've knew

What if you went to a party, and the only thing you saw was dip?

Mr. Crum George is responsible for the potato chip

Did you check your mail today?

Phillip Downing's mailbox paved the way

Garrett Morgan saves many with the gas mask from toxic pickles

And prevented many car crashes as well with his traffic signal

Latimer Lewis gave us better light with a carbon filament

Richard Spikes freed up hand space with his automatic gearshift

It's a hot summer and the kids are playing Batman and Joker

The kids need toy weapons, give them Lonnie
Johnson's super soaker

You have much more,

I read a black man invented the guitar

From the Torpedo

To help win naval wars

To open heart surgery

The refrigerator to synthetic chemistry

We are part of American history

Scary Asses

Thank you for my Fore Fathers and Mothers

No reference to Rushmore

Malcolm, Huey, Assata, and Afeni Shakur

They put their lives on the line

They wanted more

Not just reparations, education, and healthcare

They gave us WIC, free breakfast, and black welfare

Only to be called terrorist

To be called thug

Because they were proud to be black

They acknowledged our love

Only because we found ways

Rather we knew the formula on how to take care of ourselves

We just wanted the day to seize

We're sitting on the shelves

They want us to rely on them

They want us to depend on them

But they threw us in the lake when we couldn't swim

We don't want your float, nope!

We have our strong heroes

They said Obama was our change

But they still refer us as niggers and Negroes

We don't need them and we are not their dogs

We will not be man's best friends to greedy hogs

We want our own we want to grow

Simply get out the way

Let us be, so our progress will not be slowed

Our production and our progression

Our inventions and miracles

Even though its mustard through oppression

My Politics

My first President was W. Jr.

Well, technically Honest Abe

He freed the slaves

Then we can fast forward to JFK

Not to mention Billy Clinton

...Wait a motha-fucking minute

I take all of that back

Number one, for my people is JFK

Because of a Honest Abe's paraphrase

On how he wanted to bring the North and South together

Without freeing slaves

If he could he would

Could it be the cause for the pause for our reparations?

Reparate! Reparate!

The shit was on pen and paper

You breached that contract

No honesty in Honest Abe

Now Billy Clint…

Oh my goodness

My people thought this nigga was on some hood shit

Hanging around good niggas, playing saxophone

We gave him a pass

Because he would pass around some homegrown

He gets caught catching Becky

In his own home not from his wife

And we celebrate his scandal

As if this nigga is all right

???

But our people are catching false cases

1, 2, 3, the three strikes giving us life

The new slave working for good behavior with no
wage

To fill up cages

So these elites can make huge pay

And guess who has to pay?

Us!

Yes you have guessed the U.S. can be corrupt

We have a war on drugs

They're product is handed to us

Sending cops in for the big bust

One time catching us with they're stuff

The elite give us dope and false hope

They send 5-0 to your door

To take back they're dough and coke

Who's the pimp, trick, and ho?

Sad clown to black jokes

To speak of fiction that is pulp

So, when I say W. Jr. was my first

I was in reference from when I first became an adult

Let's get systematic

The patriots needed a spark to American magic

Two towers, let's crash it

Make profits on American flags and caskets

Drive up the prices of gas

And name it The Recession

Because the real money is in the Afghans

And the youth is needed to fight for Uncle Sam

Fight for freedom huh?

Please don't be dumb

We have to pay back this debt to China using opium

Producers vs. consumers, and CNN will low key flaunt it

Former CIA agents Sadam Hussein and Osama Bin Laden

America's Most Wanted

The trickledown theory

I'm at the very bottom

Had to walk through darken valleys

This is the new Sodom

I chose the half of a zip

I had to crawl high

The direction went gangster

And then came my zip line

I'm allergic to cages so I said, "fuck dope"

Then came Barry O

Time for change and hope

Uncle Sam said,

"Dude you're getting old"

"Sacrifice for me and Barry O"

"And I'll give you a new sight to a different scope"

So I swore an Oath

When the pipe's pressure busted

It wasn't for freedom

It was for my kids, In God we trusted

Get Out!

Gentrification the myth

Gentrification doesn't exist

To destroy and rebuild, it has been the formula since Plymouth

It's like an Etch a Sketch

Shake away the errors

For they created the monster

But it takes too much havoc, too much terror

When the drugs spill over the suburbs

Emergency red button, to kill the hurt

Enough!

They go from crack heads to drug victims

Justifying the test, but it's the same litmus

Number 2 pencil our water

But we're given the water bill

But the filters work fine just right over the hills

Of course they want us to be moved out

Through a new route to the same mouse trap

Amazing the maze, to be played, Uncle Sam's pimp slap

Turn your house into a Starbucks

Bring in the privileged spending kids

Brought to you by Daddy Warbucks

The rich stay rich

Plymouth Thieves

Brotha Malcolm, Brotha Malcolm, tragic the outcome

Checkmate is the game, for they sent our own

Digging deep of claws, dirty birds to falcons

To put holes in the flesh

In front of your family

The need to neutralize

Because you opened too many eyes

You gave us a blueprint

A formulated agenda

Teaching us self-discipline

To protect our placentas

That we were never lazy or inferior

We don't own dimensions of dementia

Impaired reasoning

Brotha Malcolm, Brotha Malcolm

Thank you for your wisdom

Thank you for your knowledge

Inspired more to read

For you to bleed, only so we can breathe

To show us the need to overcome Plymouth Thieves

Ass Backwards

When we are very quick to pull out the so-called stick

Annihilate our own skin

Eliminate our foes, 9 times out of 10 it was over a hoe

Now let's not take nothing away

From all the dismay the racists' cops have displayed

Plus the KKK

But I'm talking to, and referring in reference to us

Why are we so ass backwards?

We become "bar none," if another "nigga" disses our sister, disses our mom

But then we let this gun and badge

Snatch up and grab mom by the hair, and throw sister in the cab

Batons to the ribs giving lightweight jabs

And we do nothing?

Oh! We pulled out our phones, and pushed record, as if we are doing something

This is when that confused brave brother goes on a killing spree

At a march that was supposed to be peacefully

Killing cops that didn't deserve to be a part of that history

Probably killed a few that had some decency

Along while the racist pigs on the force continue to exterminate thee

Only because we are programmed to kill our own

Might as well give us a pillow case

With two holes and a white robe

PTSD

I suffer from PTSD, and short spells of anxiety

"But I'm wearing my seat belt", saying to myself

Why is this cop behind me?

We were going in two different opposite directions

But from the jump he was eyeing me

"Dear Lord, not today"

I don't want to be a crime scene

Red and blue flashing lights

And also the flash light in my face blinding me

For crying out loud!

But I have to be smart, so myself I silence me

He will push my buttons, gears will be grinding

It's the art of studying pussies... Gynecology

This isn't the so-called "good cop"

He was simply profiling me

Stanza 3

Why don't we bring back the third stanza?

No refuge could save the hireling and slave

Will everyone still stand?

They took it out for a reason

We have an amended right to take a knee

But they say its treason

The contradictions of disrespecting soldiers

Saying they died for you to stand

Understand they did both

You can't tell me I don't love my country, my soil

But it's not just freedom

It's for resources like oil

That commander and chief tries to rule this mixed soup

But wants to add salt and beef

Where half of the soil is divided and duped

Get the chef out the kitchen

Ignorant statement, ignorant intentions

The cancer, the blemish making this country sick

I'm ashamed, we shame and black ball Kaepernick

Is it because he gives a damn about American existence?

Again,

What's up with that third stanza?

ASSATA

Assata

They can say what you did

But will not say what they have done

Ready to pass a heavy bid

They called you the "Mother Hen"

They say it was you who provoked

The be comer of the bullshit

They forbade you to 2nd amend

To carry a gun

Let's not speak on their ways to infiltrate mixed
with their corruption

It's about what you did, not what they have done

Can you believe what they had to say?

They said you attempted a robbery at the Statler
Hotel

And that you robbed a bank in Queens

A bank in the Bronx too

Kidnapped James Freeman

Murdered Richard Nelson

They will like to say you have multiple attempts of murdering policemen

The shootout at a turnpike

Why, oh why

The reason for the season

To give them a reaction

If we rise, we face being labeled heathen

Mr. Gaye's "What's going on"?

Only one could hold

Three dismissals, three acquittals, but only one conviction

No matter the plea

One way or another

They wanted to get you

To do away with our queen

But they refuse to say what they have done

Beaten and caged

Tortured trying to break our mother Earth

I read with rage

Our protector of life

For this heavenly bird needed to be freed

America's most wanted

Away to Cuba

For political asylum

Let Assata rest

She has done more than her best

We are not created that solid anymore

Last of a dying

All power to the people

Paid vacation

They lay us down to the ground

You know your rights

You try not to make a sound

To provoke us

They win the first round

Just another ploy to bring you down

To take away from your crown

Your arm given a twist

An awkward bend to your wrist

Violated with a dig and frisk

Nothing comfortable, in addition to pain

They have the nerve to say, "Don't resist!"

What kind of mind fuck is this?

Ok, let's say you do everything right

The fact that it was a DWB

Your pride is stern, but remain polite

They still feel they're above your rights

And if you sneeze, it's the trigger squeeze

Because they said "We're in fear of our lives"

In broad daylight hands up in plain sight

Four different camera angles

Open and shut case for murder 1, right?

He said he mistook your car keys as a knife

Your phone looked like a gun

You weren't even running

You were just nervous of his commands and couldn't understand

Because he had you do the Hokie Poky mixed in with a Diddy dance

"Take that, Take that"

So now you're shot on the ground flat

For having your hands up, but now he orders "Hands behind your back!"

Apparently you're bleeding out

Because if you're dead, your side of the story, no statement out your mouth

Hesitation on the EMT

Life support, no need

The plan is for you to die on the scene

So what's left?

The stall out

You have to wait for trial

Wait for justice

Be patient

While these racists ass pigs get leave with paid vacation

Acre and Mule

They tell us to move on

Get over it

But the binding contract of the 13th, 14th, and 15th Amendment states

You owe us poker chips

It's like a flooded urinal

And got dammit we're over pissed

The older we get, and things still remain, we will not remain over with

Reparations "reparate" us

Remember, we're dumb

We are going to spend it up on rims and Timbs, and not land and guns

Isn't that what makes you afraid? Huh?

Because "some" niggas are smart

Television programs the brain

But it doesn't place tame on the heart

Stop it, please!

What are you fishing for?

Tuna? Cat? Carp?

Are you scared obtaining land and guns is how a race war will start?

"Reparate" us our reparations

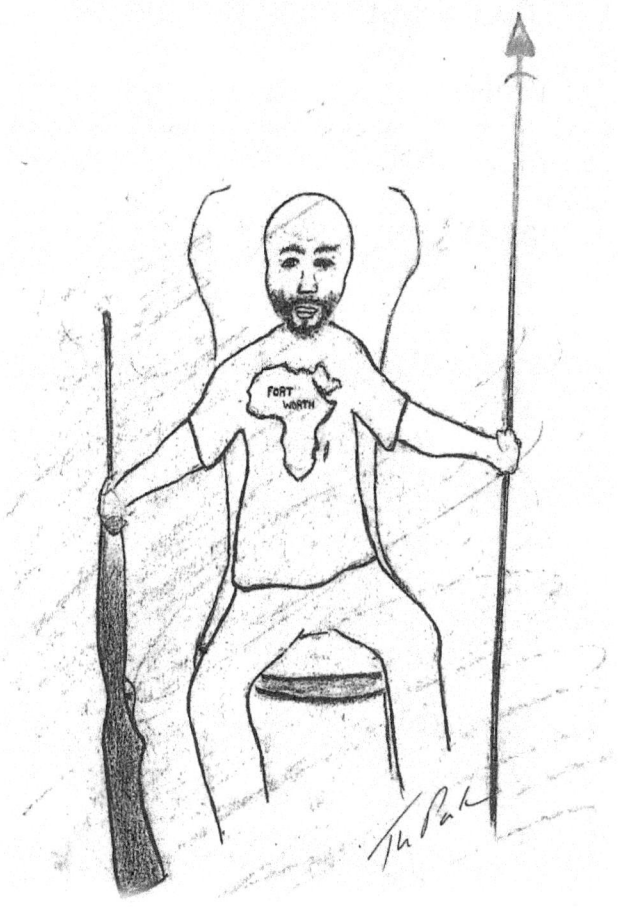

We Need More Huey's

You knew that your life was on the line

You knew this revolution would be suicide

But still your words were spoken

Slap the sandman

So we could be woken

Give us hope and

Much more

To us you were bigger than the pope

The government's uproar

One of our saviors

Teaching to love your neighbor

And to put a foot in the ass

Of these so called black skin haters

Teaching us to not ask for favors

The only thing we wanted

Was for them to stay out of our way

And to put the Ten Point program into play

To be free, to be employed

The white capitalist

Should be the ones to avoid

Freedom for all

Even if it took a black wall

We need more Huey's

Huey wanted us to read

For us to be smart

To know your rights when encountering law enforcement

Be proud, have heart

Education is where it starts

The ability to read

Knowledge grows us all

The necessity we need

Assed Out

Pull your pants up young potna

We know it was a trend

Nothing lasts forever

It's time to say The End

The end to dumb nigga shit

Let's end this house niggas vs. the niggas in the field

To blend brings confusion, the weapon and the shield

I mean, why are we showing our asses anyways?

Why do we over indulge on pills?

Tears of a clown, they laugh at us

The sad feeling to feel

It was we!

We taught them how to cook

We gave them hygiene

If it wasn't the Moors, It was Egyptian kings and queens

And now they have flipped us, everything is flipped

Dominant traits from God

Through examples of music and athletics

From science to math

Inventions, art, and aesthetics

And you mean to tell me you don't want to king up?

You scared to be God body?

Pull your pants up young potna

Self-Reflection

My ambitions to ride

Chase away unnecessary pride

Conquer the prevention of my demise

Listen and hear my people's cries

They're tears of a sad clown

Foolish wants foolish needs

Brainwashed

But the tears repel to beads

Mandatory moments

Because we see the living

Of the happily ever after

Thrown into life

With no head start

Our scattered chapters

It's like a Spike Lee Joint

Or a Tarantino flick

Life's mixtures of good music and hard truths

Blood, sweat, and shit

Constipated strains and popping veins

Tic for tac fighting over squares

-2 ply

El Fin

Forgive me for my author's portrait. I was limited civilian attire. *Love n Politics* was not planned, but I am thankful the outcome. I am thankful of everything in my life including all regrets and mistakes made. Everything is art. Everything is love. Numbers are the accurate truth. Pass my energy around.

Love n Politics: Part 2 (Coming Soon)

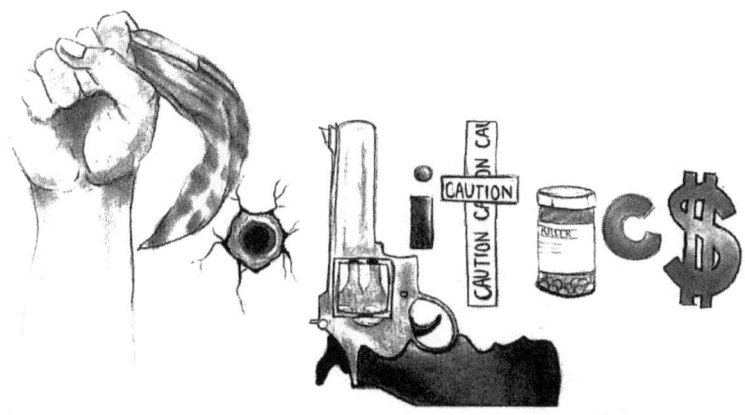